GRIZZLY BEARS

BY RACHEL HAMBY

Copyright © 2023 by Apex Editions, Mendota Heights, MN 55120. All rights reserved. No part of this book may be reproduced or utilized in any form or by any means without written permission from the publisher.

Apex is distributed by North Star Editions:
sales@northstareditions.com | 888-417-0195

Produced for Apex by Red Line Editorial.

Photographs ©: Shutterstock Images, cover, 1, 4–5, 6, 8–9, 12, 13, 14–15, 18–19, 20, 24; iStockphoto, 7, 10–11, 16–17, 22–23, 26–27, 29

Library of Congress Control Number: 2022910612

ISBN
978-1-63738-442-8 (hardcover)
978-1-63738-469-5 (paperback)
978-1-63738-520-3 (ebook pdf)
978-1-63738-496-1 (hosted ebook)

Printed in the United States of America
Mankato, MN
012023

TABLE OF CONTENTS

CHAPTER 1

CATCHING A MEAL

A grizzly bear splashes through the river. It watches for fish. It stops above a small waterfall.

Grizzly bears are good at swimming short distances.

Grizzlies catch salmon as the fish swim upstream.

Suddenly, a salmon leaps from the water. The bear catches the salmon in its mouth. Its jaws crush the fish's **skull**.

FAST FACT

Some grizzlies use their sharp claws to catch fish. The claws can grow 4 inches (10 cm) long.

Grizzlies use their long claws to grip, dig, and climb.

The bear takes its catch to the **riverbank**. It eats the salmon. Then it goes back into the water to catch another fish.

WATCH AND LEARN

Bear cubs sometimes watch their mothers catch fish. Mothers bring their cubs part of the meat. That helps the cubs learn. Soon, they can catch their own fish.

A grizzly bear can eat as many as 40 salmon in one day.

CHAPTER 2

BIG BROWN BEAR

Grizzly bears are a type of brown bear. Full-grown grizzlies often weigh more than 500 pounds (227 kg). And they can stand 9 feet (3 m) tall.

A grizzly bear's fur can be light or dark brown.

Many grizzly bears can be found in Alaska and Canada.

Grizzly bears live in North America. They live in mountains, forests, and grasslands. Many grizzlies stay near rivers or streams.

STRONG BODIES

A grizzly bear has a hump on its back. This hump is made of muscle. Grizzlies use their strong muscles to dig. They dig to make **dens** and find food.

A grizzly bear's hump is by its shoulders.

Grizzly bears usually live alone. But sometimes, several bears hunt in the same **territory**. They may even eat food side by side.

Sometimes, many grizzlies gather to catch salmon.

FAST FACT

Grizzlies can live up to 30 years in the wild.

CHAPTER 3

FINDING FOOD

Grizzly bears eat many different things. They are **omnivores**. They often eat berries, roots, and nuts.

Grizzly bears can eat up to 30 pounds (14 kg) of food a day.

Grizzlies also eat meat. They hunt large and small animals. Grizzlies have strong senses of smell. They are fast, too. They can run 35 miles per hour (56 km/h) to catch **prey**.

Grizzlies can smell dead animals from miles away.

PEOPLE PROBLEMS

Grizzly bears don't have many predators. But humans are a threat to them. People move into areas where bears live. They build roads that split up bear habitats. Cars can hit grizzlies, too.

In warm months, grizzly bears eat and eat. They build up fat to prepare for winter.

FAST FACT

A grizzly bear may gain up to 400 pounds (181 kg) to get ready for winter.

Male grizzly bears are usually bigger than females.

CHAPTER 4

SURVIVING WINTER

Grizzly bear habitats are very cold in the winter. Food is scarce and hard to find. So, grizzlies rest inside dens.

During winter, ice and snow cover the ground in many places where grizzly bears live.

When grizzlies rest, their heartbeats and breathing slow down. This helps the bears save energy. They can go months without eating or drinking.

A COZY HOME

Grizzlies make new dens every fall. First, they dig holes in the ground. Then, they add branches and leaves. These beddings keep the dens warm during winter.

Grizzlies sleep the most in winter. But they rest during the day in summer, too.

Grizzly bear cubs are usually born in winter. They leave the dens in spring with their mothers. Mother bears care for their cubs for about two years. Then the young bears go live on their own.

FAST FACT

Grizzly bears stay in their dens for five to seven months.

Grizzly mothers usually have one to four cubs at a time.

COMPREHENSION QUESTIONS

Write your answers on a separate piece of paper.

1. Write a few sentences describing how grizzly bears catch fish.

2. Grizzly bears eat many things. What is your favorite food? Why do you like it?

3. What time of year are grizzly bear cubs born?

    A. spring

    B. summer

    C. winter

4. How would watching their mother help cubs learn to hunt?

    A. The cubs can find their mother's smell.

    B. The cubs can copy their mother's actions.

    C. The cubs can steal their mother's food.

5. What does **threat** mean in this book?

Grizzly bears don't have many predators. But humans are a threat to them.

 A. help
 B. danger
 C. food

6. What does **scarce** mean in this book?

Grizzly bear habitats are very cold in the winter. Food is scarce and hard to find.

 A. growing everywhere
 B. not common
 C. easy to get

Answer key on page 32.

GLOSSARY

dens
The homes of wild animals.

habitats
The places where animals normally live.

omnivores
Animals that eat both plants and animals.

predators
Animals that hunt and eat other animals.

prey
Animals that are hunted and eaten by other animals.

riverbank
Land at the edge of a river.

skull
The bones of the head that surround and protect the brain.

territory
An area that an animal or group of animals lives in and defends.

TO LEARN MORE

BOOKS

Murray, Julie. *Fun Facts About Bears*. Minneapolis: Abdo Publishing, 2022.

Murray, Julie. *Grizzly Bears*. Minneapolis: Abdo Publishing, 2020.

Sommer, Nathan. *Grizzly Bear vs. Wolf Pack*. Minneapolis: Bellwether Media, 2020.

ONLINE RESOURCES

Visit **www.apexeditions.com** to find links and resources related to this title.

ABOUT THE AUTHOR

Rachel Hamby writes poetry, fiction, and nonfiction for kids. She lives in Washington State with her husband, corgi, and kids.

INDEX

C
claws, 7
cubs, 8, 26

D
dens, 13, 22, 25–27
dig, 13, 25

F
forests, 12

G
grasslands, 12

H
habitat, 19, 22
hump, 13
hunt, 14, 18

M
mountains, 12

O
omnivores, 16

P
predators, 19
prey, 18

R
rest, 22, 25
river, 4, 12

T
territory, 14

W
winter, 21, 22, 25–26

ANSWER KEY:
1. Answers will vary; 2. Answers will vary; 3. C; 4. B; 5. B; 6. B